Humble Bee

A
Story
about
Pride

Written and Illustrated by Matt Whitlock

www.cookcommunications.com/kidz

A Faith Parenting Guide
can be found on page 32.

Faith Kidz® is an imprint of Cook Communications Ministries
Colorado Springs, Colorado 80918
Cook Communications, Paris, Ontario
Kingsway Communications, Eastbourne, England

HUMBLEBEE
©2003 by Matthew Whitlock for text and illustrations

First printing, 2003
Printed in Singapore
1 2 3 4 5 6 7 8 9 10 Printing/Year 07 06 05 04 03

Senior Editor: Heather Gemmen
Design Manager: Jeffrey P. Barnes
Designer: Granite Design

Library of Congress Cataloging-in-Publication Data

Whitlock, Matt.
  Humblebee / by Matt Whitlock.
      p. cm.
  Summary: Bee's head swells up to a frightening size when he boasts
dishonestly about his skill as a baker.
  ISBN 0-7814-3831-4
  [1. Conduct of life--Fiction. 2. Bees--Fiction. 3. Stories in rhyme.]
  I. Title.
  PZ8.3.W595 Hu 2002
  [E]--dc21
                                        2002001151

This book is
dedicated to
John

Many thanks to:
Jenny, Mary McNeil, Heather Gemmen, Carrie Greno, Eva Marie Everson,
Mike Vandemark, Will Briggs, Jeff & Julia Gilbert, Maman et Mojo

There once lived a sad bee who couldn't make honey–
he never learned how to in school.
He ran a small snack shop that made him no money
and thus made him feel like a fool.

This way to...
BEE'S
SNACK SHOP

I ASSURE YOU
WE'RE
OPEN!

FLY-THRU
service

4

A sweet girl named Sunni passed by him one day
and, knowing that bee stings can smart,
she walked to the sad-looking bee anyway
because of her kind, tender heart.

BEE-LICIOUS HONEY

To cheer up the bee, Sunni gave him a present:
some honey she had from her luncheon.
Bee tried some and found it was much more than pleasant–
that honey was heavenly munchin'!

Bee's
SNACK SHOP

Sorry! We have
NO HONEY!

She left him the jar and then skipped down the road.
Bee dashed to the pots on his racks.
He whipped up some sweet honey pie a-la-mode
and cooked the world's best honey snacks.

NOW SERVING
NUMBER:

0524 19750202-
19770S 12 1978-
0225 198 10 124-
19474078270455

MILLIONS OF SATISFIED
INSECTS SERVED

The next day bugs came—some were young, some were old—
the richest as well as the poorest.
They all wanted some of that honey-sweet gold.
Bee's shop was the talk of the forest!

Please...
TAKE A
NUMBER

11

Ant begged for the secret to Bee's big success.
Bee started to tell him of Sunni–
but wanting all credit, he didn't confess
the source of his dee-licious honey.

Ant watched as Bee's head grew as big as a peach—
it grew as Bee bragged of his riches.
(I'm not saying this like a figure of speech,
like "You are too big for your britches!")

The ant was so frightened,
he ran away yelling.
The puzzled bee didn't quite get it.

16

He didn't understand
that his head started swelling
each time he took
all of the credit.

WE NOW HAVE HONEY!
...the greatest honey you ever tasted, thanks to the unbelievable
genius of yours truly. BEE

A spider applied for a job at the store,
but Bee said, "Don't bother, I'm fine!
Though your hands outnumber my bee hands times four,
the best hands for baking are mine!"

Embrassez
le Chef

Bee's head kept on growing–
and not just a bit.
Soon all of Bee's friends
felt neglected.
He cared not for them–
but he cared when he hit
a problem that wasn't
expected.

DEE-LICIOUS

The bee soon discovered his jar was bone dry;
and then to his utter dismay–
he called out for help, but no bugs heard his cry.
He'd pushed all his good friends away.

21

Bee needed to fill up his big honey pot
in order to keep making money.
He grabbed for the jar and he hatched a great plot
to search for the kind girl named Sunni.

He found the girl picnicking
out in some clover.
She turned and she saw his big head.
Bee gave her the jar,
but she nearly keeled over
and screamed till her face
turned bright red!

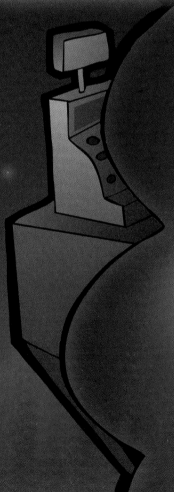

Bee slowly buzzed home, then he sat down and cried.
His life had now sunk to its worst.
He figured it must have been due to his pride—
he hadn't put other folks first.

24

A wonderful thing happened there at the store
as Bee did some praying and thinking.
His head shrank back down to the same as before–
his humbleness caused all the shrinking!

A ladybug noticed a change in Bee's mood—
his bragging had come to a stop.
She went to her home and she baked up some food
so Bee could reopen his shop.

T he bee told her thank you, then had to reveal
he didn't work well as a loner.
He asked her to work there, then offered a deal:
her job would be as the new owner!

29

The snack shop reopened with hoopla and hype.
Big signs hung through all of the trees.

See

Lady's **NEW**

SNACK SHOP

. . . it read in large type.

In small print it said,

(... and Bee's)

HumbleBee

Ages: 4-7
Life Issue: I want my children to enjoy being who God made them to be.
Spiritual Building Block: Humility

Do the following activities to help your children develop a healthy sense of humility:

SIGHT: Humility does not mean degrading ourselves; humility means knowing who we are in relation to God. Help your children to discover how mighty God is by reading Bible stories that describe him. Read the description of God in Revelation 4:2–6 to your children and ask them to draw a picture of what you've read. Tell them to imagine how wonderful and frightening it would be to walk up to God on his throne.

SOUND: Since humility is knowing who we are in relation to God, tell your children many stories about how much God loves them. Read the stories of the lost sheep, the lost coin, and the lost son (Luke 15). Emphasize how incredible it is that our mighty God gave up so much because he loves us. Thank God together for treasuring us even though we're so tiny compared to him.

TOUCH: Once they understand who they are in relation to God, your kids will begin to understand who they are in relation to others. Grab a stack of magazines and ask your kids to cut out pictures of all the people God loves. Tell them that since God loves each of us equally, we cannot think we are better (or worse) than anyone. Pray with your children that God will help them, and all the people in their collage, to choose to put God first.